DEEP SEA EXPLORATION

Richard Spilsbury

Crabtree Publishing Company

www.crabtreebooks.com

Author: Richard Spilsbury
Editor: Kathy Middleton
Production coordinator: Ken Wright
Prepress technician: Margaret Amy Salter
Series consultant: Gill Matthews

Picture Credits:

Corbis: Jeffrey Rotman (Cover) 7, Denis Scott 18, Paul Souders 9t
FLPA: Luciano Candisani/Minden Pictures 17
Fotolia: Kurt De Bruyn 28, Richard Carey 10, 13t, Juergen Rudorf 9b, Ilan Ben Tov 21
Istockphoto: Geoffrey Hollman 4–32, Jodi Jacobson 8
NOAA: 13b, 22b, 27, Ian MacDonald, Texas A & M University, Corpus Christi 24, National Undersea Research Program (NURP) 29t, OAR/NURP 25, OAR/NURP/University of Connecticut 26, OAR/NURP/Woods Hole Oceanographic Institute 29b
Photoshot: NHPA 5
Rex Features: 20
Shutterstock: Anton Bryksin 19t, A Cotton Photo 4, Grivina 4–32, Lijuan Guo 16t, Ivanova Inga 19b, Bill Kennedy 16b, Mana Photo 22t, Niar 15t, Sergey Popov V 14, Roman & Olexandra 12, Ian Scott 11t, Elisei Shafer 15b, Morozova Tatyana (Manamana) 6, 11b
Illustrations: Geoff Ward

Library and Archives Canada Cataloguing in Publication

Spilsbury, Richard, 1963-
  Deep sea exploration / Richard Spilsbury.

(Crabtree connections)
Includes index.
ISBN 978-0-7787-9893-4 (bound).--ISBN 978-0-7787-9914-6 (pbk.)

       1. Underwater exploration--Juvenile literature. I. Title. II. Series:
Crabtree connections

GC65.S65 2010   j551.46   C2010-905076-2

Library of Congress Cataloging-in-Publication Data

Spilsbury, Richard, 1963-
  Deep sea exploration / Richard Spilsbury.
    p. cm. -- (Crabtree connections)
  Includes index.
  ISBN 978-0-7787-9914-6 (pbk. : alk. paper) -- ISBN 978-0-7787-9893-4 (reinforced library binding : alk. paper)
  1. Underwater exploration--Juvenile literature. I. Title.
  GC65.S72 2011
  551.46--dc22
                              2010030827

Crabtree Publishing Company

Printed in the U.S.A./082010/WO20101210

Published in Canada
Crabtree Publishing
616 Welland Ave.
St. Catharines, Ontario
L2M 5V6

Published in the United States
Crabtree Publishing
PMB 59051
350 Fifth Avenue, 59th Floor
New York, New York 10118

CONTENTS

SECRETS OF THE DEEP

Deep beneath the blue surface of the oceans lies an inky-black world. Some of the most fascinating creatures on Earth have been found in these dark, icy depths. Many more, yet undiscovered, may live here. Our mission is to journey to this underwater world to find them. Are you ready for the trip of a lifetime?

Bottlenose dolphins swim in groups near the ocean surface.

What did we find?

Underwater mountains

Scientists have determined that the ocean floor is smooth and flat in some areas, but covered in underwater mountains in others. Some of these mountains are thousands of feet (meters) high, yet some do not even stick out of the water!

Weird and wonderful creatures, such as this hatchet fish, live in the deep waters of the world's oceans.

THE RIGHT EQUIPMENT

If we try to dive down to the ocean's deepest parts in our wetsuits, the **pressure** would crush our lungs! Instead, we will travel in a **submersible**—a diving machine designed for the deep sea.

Look for our submersible on the following pages. It will show how deep we are.

Sunlight zone	0-656 ft (0-200 m), plenty of light
Twilight zone	656-3280 ft (200-1000 m), a little light
Midnight zone	3280-13,123 ft (1000-4000 m), hardly any light
Dark zone	13,123-16,404 ft (4000-5000+ m), no light

trench

OUR SCUBA KIT

- A wetsuit protects a diver from cold water, but not from deep sea pressure.
- An air tank provides oxygen for a few hours, but not long enough to travel deep below.
- Flippers help a diver swim farther, but not for hundreds of feet (meters).

The deeper underwater you go, the greater pressure there is. **Scuba** divers can only dive safely to about 164 feet (50 meters).

Our submersible has

- thick steel walls to withstand the high pressures of the deep sea;
- a tough but thin crystal window instead of thick glass;
- big compressed air tanks: 8 gallons (30 liters) per person per minute, plus more in case of emergency;
- propellers to move us in different directions underwater;
- lights and cameras;
- "grab arms" to pick up deep-sea samples.

A submersible looks a little bit like an armored spacecraft!

FEEDING FRENZY

We sink beneath the ocean's surface in our submersible. Right away we see a turtle slowly swimming by and then a large, shimmering school of small fish.

Predators and prey

The fish had been eating **plankton**, which are tiny floating plant-like animals. But now they were being attacked. Seabirds were diving into the water to peck at the fish. Large tuna fish, dolphins, sea lions, and even a humpback whale were swimming into the **shoal** to catch their **prey**. This was an ocean feeding frenzy!

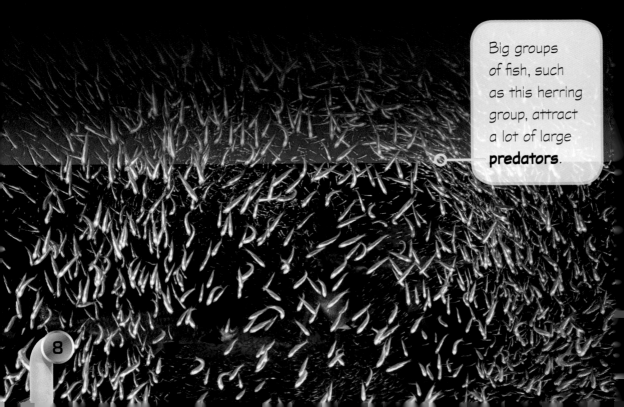

Big groups of fish, such as this herring group, attract a lot of large **predators**.

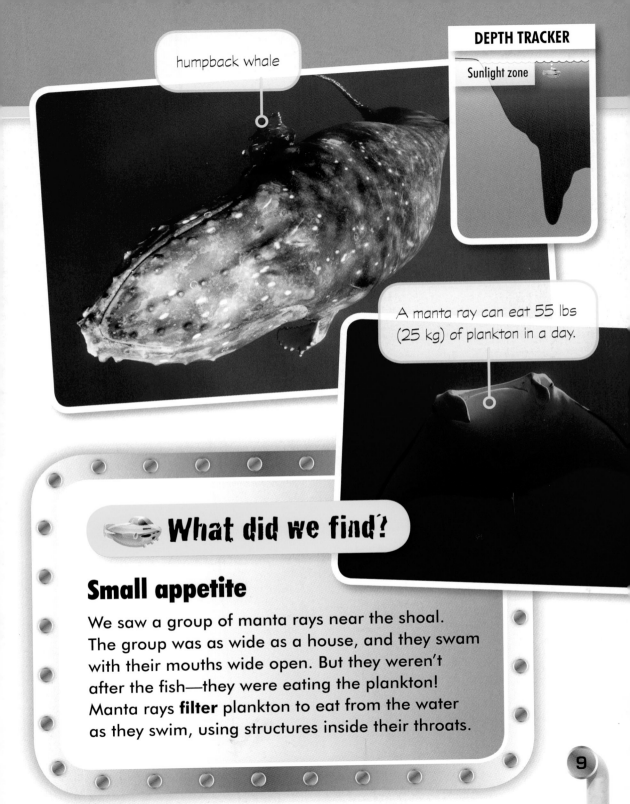

humpback whale

Sunlight zone

A manta ray can eat 55 lbs (25 kg) of plankton in a day.

What did we find?

Small appetite

We saw a group of manta rays near the shoal. The group was as wide as a house, and they swam with their mouths wide open. But they weren't after the fish—they were eating the plankton! Manta rays **filter** plankton to eat from the water as they swim, using structures inside their throats.

REEF LIFE

An hour later a reef shark surprises us while we are swimming outside the submersible to look at a **coral reef** in shallow water. The shark swims close enough for us to look into its black eyes and check out its sharp teeth.

Underwater community

The reef is home to an underwater community. We see seastars feeding on the coral and colorful fish nibbling on seaweeds. One section of reef appears to move. Then I realize it is not part of the reef, but is actually an octopus!

An octopus can change its skin color to match the area where it is hiding.

reef shark

Corals grow in many different shapes and colors.

What did we find?

Coral reef

Reefs can look like strange rocky plants, but they are made up of animals called coral polyps. They build hard coral shelters around their bodies in light, warm seawater. The coral builds up over many years to create reefs. Reefs look tough but they are fragile and easily damaged. We were very careful as we swam back to the submersible.

SHIPWRECK!

As we drop towards the seafloor, we see the wreck of a ship. At the front there is a jagged hole. We guess that the ship may have sunk because it hit the reef.

scallop

 ## What did we find?

Seafloor life

A spider crab was crawling along the seafloor near the shipwreck, balancing on its long legs. The mud of the seafloor is full of life, which is tasty food for some creatures. Sure enough, the spider crab found some scallops. They looked like swimming false teeth as they tried to escape!

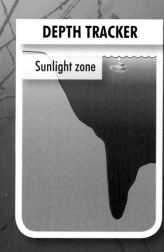

Sunlight zone

There are about three million shipwrecks in the oceans around the world.

Frozen in time

We peer inside the ship through the windows. It is like it has been frozen in time. One cabin has a picture on the wall, half-covered by a seastar. In another room we see broken dishes, tins of food, and a stove, all with yellow **sponges** clinging to them

The *Titanic* is one of the most famous of all shipwrecks.

13

EEL ENCOUNTER

As we swim past the hole in the shipwreck, a pointed face pokes out, with its mouth wide open. It is an eel. We watch as its long, spotted body turns and swims back into the gloom of the ship.

Safe inside

Shoals of big, bullet-shaped barracuda fish are hunting for food outside the wreck. We see that other fish stayed inside. Shipwrecks are a bit like **artificial** reefs. There are a lot of hiding places for animals to keep out of the way of predators. Sea horses slowly move among the corals, sponges, and weeds that have grown on the ship.

Barracudas are fast-swimming fish with razor-sharp teeth.

Moray eels often rest with their mouths open. This helps them breathe.

 What did we find?

Poisonous lion

The lion fish is only about 12 inches (30 cm) long, but it came right up to the submersible. It is a beautiful striped fish with lots of long, pointed spines. It was unafraid because its spines are weapons. If one jabbed you, it would really hurt and make you very ill.

TWILIGHT ZONE

We press our faces to the glass of a side window and look into the dark. We can see the flashing lights of cuttlefish and sea jellies. The rounded top of one sea jelly looks like it's at least 6 feet (2 m) across. Thank goodness we are inside the submersible and out of reach of all those stinging tentacles.

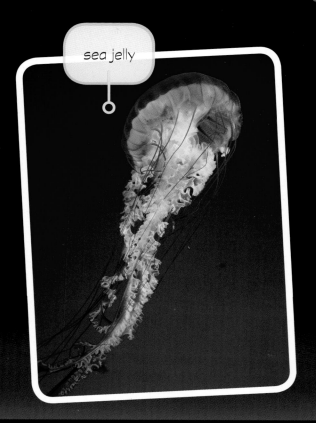

sea jelly

Cuttlefish send messages to each other by flashing light in the dark.

Deeper and darker

We have reached the twilight zone of the ocean about one-third of a mile (1/2 km) down. Only a tiny amount of sunlight can reach these depths. Outside the temperature is dropping and the pressure is rising as we go deeper.

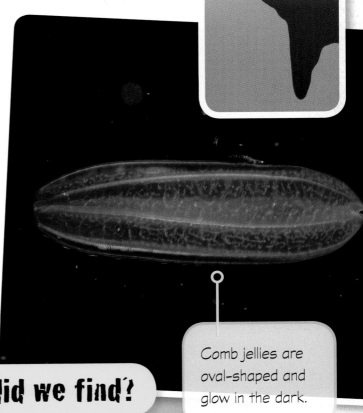

Comb jellies are oval-shaped and glow in the dark.

What did we find?

Lighting up the deep

Many deep sea animals produce their own light. Chemicals in their bodies mix and react to release light, just like glow sticks do. The animals make light for different reasons. Some use light to find their way in the dark, others to attract mates or to draw prey closer so they can eat them.

BATTLE OF THE GIANTS

At 2,600 feet (800 m) deep there is a huge whack on the side of the submersible. We rush to look through the window and see a giant squid! Its **tentacles** are trying to grip onto the submersible. This animal must be 32 feet (10 m) long.

Squid hunter!

Then, an even bigger shape appears fast out of the darkness. It is a sperm whale, and it is hunting the squid. The squid tries to get away, but the whale grabs it firmly.

Sperm whales can stay underwater for more than two hours.

What did we find?

Swimming deep

Whales need to breathe air to survive. A whale takes many huge gulps of air before it dives. It stores most of the oxygen from the air in its muscles and blood.

SQUID EYES

A giant squid's eyes can be as big as soccer balls! They are like headlights to help the squid see in the dark.

DEEP-SEA SURVIVORS

We eventually reach deep, black water. We come across an angler fish. The tip of the antenna above its mouth looks like a wiggling piece of tasty food. The angler fish is also lit up. It is ready to snap up any fish attracted by this clever trick.

Adapted for eating

There is not much food for animals down here, so predators need special features to help them survive in the dark. The angler fish has its light. The deep sea gulper has wide jaws. It can fit a much larger animal than itself in its mouth.

Most angler fish are only the size of a person's fist.

Midnight zone

Sea cucumbers chew up any pieces of dead animals that fall to the ocean floor.

What did we find?

Deep-sea suckers

We saw strange marks, a little like tire tracks, across the ocean floor. We realized that sea cucumbers were leaving tracks as they slowly moved along. Sea cucumbers suck up mud from the ocean floor into their stomachs, to extract any hidden bits of food that might be in the mud.

SHOCK IN THE OCEAN

Without any warning the submersible suddenly lurches to the side and is out of control. It tumbles against a rock and the lights go off for a moment. It must be an underwater earthquake!

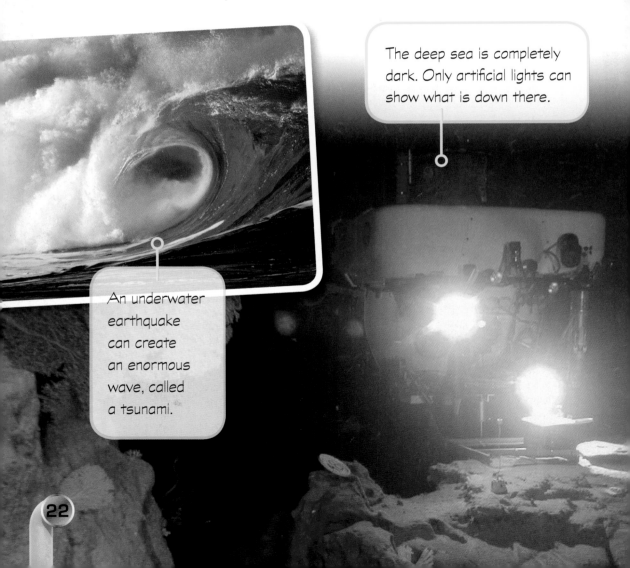

The deep sea is completely dark. Only artificial lights can show what is down there.

An underwater earthquake can create an enormous wave, called a tsunami.

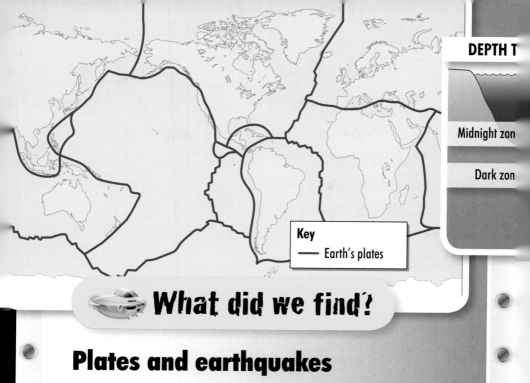

Midnight zon

Dark zon

Key
— Earth's plates

What did we find?

Plates and earthquakes

All the land and oceans covering Earth sit on a thick layer of rock. The layer is broken into a dozen plates that float around on slow-moving rock beneath. When plates move toward each other, they can stick and then suddenly slip beneath one another. This shakes the Earth's surface nearby, causing an earthquake.

Growing rock

We just saw some rock growing! We were at a place where plates were pulling apart. This left a crack, and liquid rock was seeping through from inside the Earth. It soon cooled down in the cold seawater and hardened. So this is how underwater mountains grow

LIVING IN THE DEPTHS

Out of the window we see pale **crabs**, **mussels**, and long red **tube worms** clustered around what looks like a chimney with black smoke coming out of it. This is a **hydrothermal vent**.

Extreme food web

The vent is hot and full of bits of dissolved rock, called **minerals**. Tiny living things, called **bacteria**, thrive there. They make food from the minerals. Mussels filter the bacteria from the water, then eat them. Crabs and other creatures feed on the mussels.

Red tube worms live near hydrothermal vents. They can grow to be taller than a person!

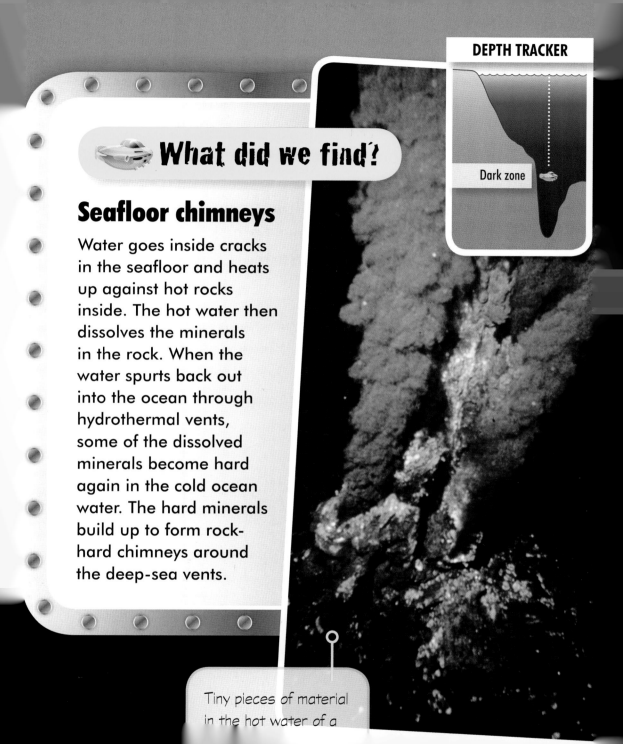

Dark zone

What did we find?

Seafloor chimneys

Water goes inside cracks in the seafloor and heats up against hot rocks inside. The hot water then dissolves the minerals in the rock. When the water spurts back out into the ocean through hydrothermal vents, some of the dissolved minerals become hard again in the cold ocean water. The hard minerals build up to form rock-hard chimneys around the deep-sea vents.

Tiny pieces of material in the hot water of a

OVER THE EDGE

Suddenly the seafloor in front of us just disappears. We have reached the edge of an ocean trench. Trenches are dips in the seafloor caused by one plate moving underneath another one. They are the deepest places on Earth.

Reaching the limit

We drop over the edge and fall fast. Soon we are 23,000 feet (7,000 m) deep. The water pressure here is 700 times greater than at the ocean's surface. The lights shine on some giant isopods—crab-like creatures that live in deep water.

This submarine has reached the bottom of a deep sea trench.

Deepest trench known

The trench we explored was small compared to the Mariana trench, near Japan. The bottom of the Mariana is around 36,100 feet (11,000 m) deep. The pressure on a submersible in a trench this deep is the same as having 48 jumbo jets stacked on it. Only one submersible with passengers has ever been taken there, and that had steel walls 5 inches (13 cm) thick.

giant isopod

DEPTH TRACKER

Dark zone

The Mariana trench was formed when two plates pushed together to create a deep cut in the seabed.

DEEP-SEA DISCOVERY

We finally return to the surface. We take with us some of the bacteria we found in the sea vents with us. This may help scientists find out more about other, harmful bacteria.

Ocean around us

As we surface, we see fishing boats pulling giant nets. People are catching so many fish that there are not many left of some species. **Trawler** nets can damage reefs and harm sea life. Scientists and fishing crews must work together to care for the oceans.

Huge amounts of fish and other sea creatures are caught in fishing boat nets.

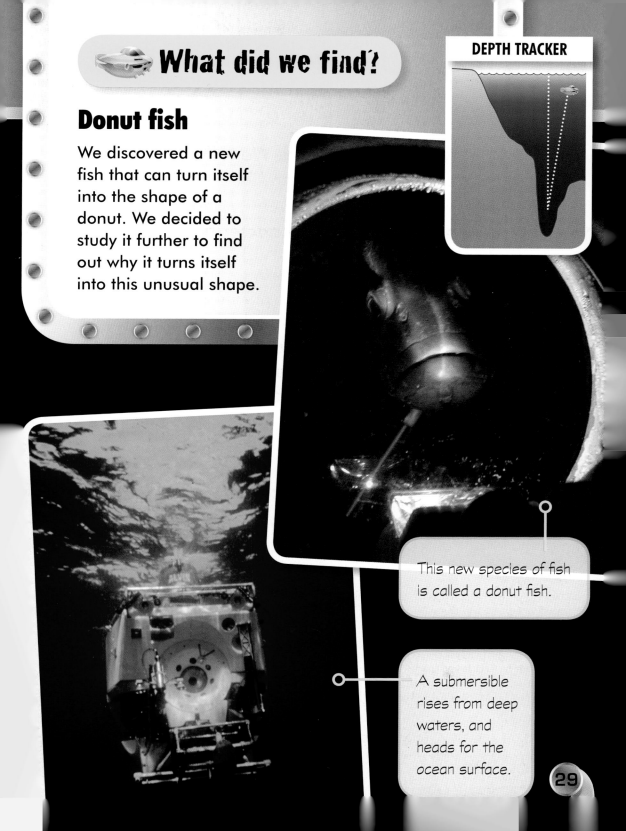

What did we find?

Donut fish

We discovered a new fish that can turn itself into the shape of a donut. We decided to study it further to find out why it turns itself into this unusual shape.

This new species of fish is called a donut fish.

A submersible rises from deep waters, and heads for the ocean surface.

29

GLOSSARY

artificial Human-made

bacteria Very simple microscopic living things

coral reef Underwater structure mainly found in warm seas, made of the skeletons of coral animals

crab Type of ten-legged animal with a tough shell, claws, and eyes on short stalks, usually found on shores or the seafloor

filter To pass liquid through a fine barrier to trap solid pieces

hydrothermal vent An opening in Earth's crust, deep beneath the ocean surface

mineral Natural substance that makes up rocks

mussel Type of animal with two hinged, long shells, mostly found on the seafloor and rocks

plankton Mixture of tiny plants and animals that drift or float through the oceans

predator Animal that hunts and eats other animals

pressure Force pressing against something, such as the force of water on someone diving

prey Animal that is eaten by other animals

SCUBA Abbreviation for "self contained underwater breathing apparatus"

shoal Shallow water

sponge Marine animals that live together in a blob-like shape with holes over the surface through which they take in food

submersible Vessel that can dive deep underwater

tentacle Long organ near the mouth of animals, including octopus and anemones, which they use to feel, feed, or grasp

trawler A boat that catches fish by dragging a huge net in the water behind it

tube worm Type of marine worm that lives in a hard tube that it makes

FURTHER INFORMATION

Web Sites

Find out more about deep-sea life at:
www.teachers.ash.org.au/jmresources/deep/creatures.html

http://deepsealife.net/

People have used all kinds of submersibles to explore the oceans. To learn more about them, visit:
www.pbs.org/wgbh/nova/abyss/frontier/deepsea.html

Would you like to know more about the world's oceans, what lives in them, and the problems they face? One place to start is:
www.panda.org/about_our_earth/blue_planet/

Books

Monsters of the Deep: Deep Sea Adaptation (Fact Finders) by Kelly Regan Barnhill. Capstone Press (2008).

Deep Sea Extremes (Extreme Nature) by Natalie Hyde. Crabtree Publishing Company (2009).

The Ocean Biome (The Living Ocean) by Kathryn Smithyman & Bobbie Kalman. Crabtree Publishing Company (2003)

Underwater Exploration (Restless Sea) by Carole Garbuny Vogel. Children's Press (2003).

INDEX